Meditations

Also by Thomas Moore

Soul Mates

Care of the Soul

Rituals of the Imagination

The Planets Within

Dark Eros

A Blue Fire: The Essential Writings of James Hillman
(Editor)

MEDITATIONS

On the Monk Who Dwells in Daily Life

Thomas Moore

HarperCollins*Publishers*

Grateful acknowledgment is made for permission to reprint excerpts from the following:

OPUS POSTHUMOUS by Wallace Stevens, edit., Samuel French Morse. Copyright © 1957 by Elsie Stevens and Holly Stevens. Reprinted by permission of Alfred A. Knopf, Inc.

"God Is Born" from THE COMPLETE POEMS OF D.H. LAWRENCE by D.H. Lawrence, edit., Vivian de Sola Pinto and Warren Roberts. Copyright © Angelo Ravagli and C.M. Weekley, Executors of The Estate of Frieda Lawrence Ravagli, 1964, 1971. Reprinted by permission of Viking Penguin, a division of Penguin Books USA Inc.

HarperCollins books may be purchased for educational, business, or sales promotional use. For information please write: Special Markets Department, HarperCollins Publishers, Inc., 10 East 53rd Street, New York, NY 10022.

FIRST EDITION

Text design and production by David Bullen
Cover design by David Bullen and Michael Katz

Library of Congress Cataloging-in-Publication Data

Moore, Thomas, 1940–
    Meditations : on the monk who dwells in daily life /
by Thomas Moore.
        p.   cm.
    ISBN 0–06–017223–1
    1. Spiritual life. 2. Monastic and religious life. 3. Moore,
Thomas, 1940–   . I. Title.
    BL624.M664   1994
    291.6′57 — dc20   94–33743

94 95 96 97 98 RRD 10 9 8 7 6 5 4 3 2 1

For Mary and Ben,
who perceived the mystery
and let it be

*W*hen I was thirteen years old I left home to enter a seminary designed to prepare young men for the Roman Catholic priesthood. I was filled with idealism and had a driving desire to aim as high as possible in my life, following the example of boys a year or two ahead of me in school whom I greatly admired. That spirit was so strong in me that it overcame the deep attachment I had felt keenly all my life to my family, to both my parents and brother at home, and my larger family of grandparents, uncles and aunts, and a host of cousins. The homesickness I felt year after year tore at my heart, and yet I stayed with the monastic regimen for twelve years. Only a few months before ordination to the priesthood I was stirred enough by the longing for a bigger world in which to live and think that I left the security of that life and began my wanderings.

The Servite Order that was family all those years had been founded in Florence, Italy, in the year 1233. It was an ancient order dedicated to the image of the sorrowful mother of Jesus. A Jungian psychologist might say that those intense years of religion had a marked anima focus, not simply on a mother figure, but specifically on a mother who suffers as a witness to her son's driven, idealistic life and torturous, disillusioned end. The community was not strictly speaking monastic, but partly contemplative and partly active—my colleagues taught in colleges and high schools and served in parishes. But even in these active settings the style of life was characterized by intense community and dedication to contemplation.

The only bad memories I have of this experience of religious life, in addition to the separation from my family, was the tendency in it toward authoritarianism. It wasn't always the case, but frequently enough I had to live under the control of "superiors" who felt it their duty to maintain strict observance of rules and customs. I've always been a sensitive person who only needs a hint of direction and a suggestion of correction. For the most part I do my rebelling in imagination, and so I didn't fare well in authoritarian atmospheres.

Otherwise, the religious life was filled with pleasures. I could live out the solitude that is part of my nature, and yet I would never be isolated—the community was always there for support and companionship. I was surrounded by men of character and good will, as well as idealism and humor. I was fortunate to be in a Catholic community that loved the world, deeply appreciated culture, and never despised earthly pleasures. Without sex, without money, and without much exercise of free will, I lived a satisfying life.

When I finally left the order, I left most of religion behind. I lived as an agnostic of sorts for a while. In my monastery days I had studied music seriously and had written and directed a considerable amount of music, and so, once out of the order, I planned on the life of an academic musician. Unexpectedly, my love of theology and religion

stayed with me. I received degrees in each field and then took up a career as a college professor, followed by many years as a psychotherapist.

With the publication of my two books, *Care of the Soul* and *Soul Mates,* in another unexpected development I received many invitations to speak in churches. I found myself in grand, lofty pulpits and on stage and in crowded bookstores talking about the soul. One time a Catholic priest on Cape Cod invited me to speak. The church was filled with people, and he insisted I speak from the pulpit. As I stood there looking at the people, the church, the pastor, and my position in the pulpit, I asked myself: "How did I get here? Here I'm doing what I hoped to do when I was thirteen. It has all come full circle. But none of it is literally as I expected it to be. This priesthood and spirituality I had sought so ardently takes form now that I have become a family man, a husband, and a writer."

Over many decades my raw thoughts and emotions about priesthood changed tone and color through an alchemy almost entirely unconscious to me, and they gathered a weight and form that I could never have predicted. In my life now both the priesthood and the monastic life are made of subtle stuff—not literal ways of life, but possibilities powdered so finely that they have become values, nuances, styles, and elements of character giving my life a certain tone and color.

This book of meditations attempts to capture that alchemy for the reader. I believe we all, men and women, have much to gain by reflecting on religious community life as a spirit that can be fostered within our ordinary, secular lives. It is a spirit that can deepen our values and experiences, nourish our souls, and reveal sacredness where one previously suspected only secularity. The meditation form is suited to this process because it is a collection of seeds, not a fully articulated conclusion, that germinate like perennial flowers in the midst of a worldly life.

These meditations come from my youthful experience of religious community and the subsequent interiorization of that experience. While our society may not seem terribly interested these days in monastic life, it is clearly hungry for a kind of spirituality that is neither divorced from ordinary life nor escapist in tone. We may not need new leaders and new philosophies as much as the recollection of old images from the past. Monasticism may appear to be dying, but that fading of a way of life offers us an unusual opportunity to regard it with increased imagination, drawing its lessons and attractions into our own lives, no matter what external shape our work and home life may take. The ghosts of the monks still speak. We have only to listen to them with subtle attentiveness.

The doings of the gods are filled with Providence.
Chance events are not unrelated to nature
    or the weaving and winding of the allotments
        of Providence.

Everything flows from Providence,
    and alongside it is Necessity,
    and whatever contributes
    to the entire universe
    of which you are a part.

Marcus Aurelius, *Meditations*

*E*ARLY CHRISTIAN MONKS WENT OUT to live in the desert in order to find emptiness. Modern life is becoming so full that we need our own ways of going to the desert to be relieved of our plenty. Our heads are crammed with information, our lives busy with activities, our cities stuffed with automobiles, our imaginations bloated on pictures and images, our relationships heavy with advice, our jobs burdened with endless new skills, our homes cluttered with gadgets and conveniences. We honor productivity to such an extent that the unproductive person or day seems a failure.

Monks are experts at doing nothing and tending the culture of that emptiness.

*M*ONASTIC BUILDINGS SHOW US how an intense interior life may generate an outward form of art, craft, and the care of things. Out of a simple life has come an extraordinary heritage of books, illuminated pages, sculpture, architecture, and music. The cultivation of the inner life overflows in outward displays of beauty and richness.

Maybe it's a mistake to think of the monastic life as a withdrawal from the active world; we might see it more as an alternative to the hyperactivity that is characteristic of modern life. Traditionally the monk is extremely active, and on many fronts: actively engaged in nurturing the inner life, actively committed to a communal style of living, and actively producing words, images, and sounds of extraordinary meaningfulness and beauty.

*I*N AN AGE OF PROFOUND CULTURAL transition, religion itself appears to be going through its own rite of passage. For some it is in a time of crisis, for others a period of vibrant change. I see religion moving toward a diminishing of dogma, authority, membership, and belief and an increase in everyday ritual, poetic theology, social engagement, guidance in contemplation, and care of the soul.

In this new setting monasticism, too, can become more a spirit than an institution, one element among several in establishing a soul-centered life, and a style that invites beauty and culture into a life of pragmatism and efficiency.

$\mathcal{W}$ITHDRAWAL FROM THE WORLD IS something we can, and perhaps should, do every day. It completes the movement of which entering fully into life is only one part. Just as a loaf of bread needs air in order to rise, everything we do needs an empty place in its interior. I especially enjoy such ordinary retreats from the active life as shaving, showering, reading, doing nothing, walking, listening to the radio, driving in a car. All of these activities can turn one's attention inward toward contemplation.

Mundane withdrawal from the busyness of an active life can create a spirituality-without-walls, a spiritual practice that is not explicitly connected to a church or a tradition. I have never forgotten Joseph Campbell's response when he was asked about his yoga practice: laps in a pool and a drink once a day. Anything is material for retreat—cleaning out a closet, giving away some books, taking a walk around the block, clearing your desk, turning off the television set, saying no to an invitation to do *anything*.

At the sight of nothing, the soul rejoices.

WHEN I LIVED IN A MONASTERY, RE-
treat from the world wasn't sufficient. One day a month
and one week each year we "went" on retreat. We didn't
leave the monastery, but we went away from it. Going
away—literally, figuratively—is the essence of retreat.

I remember a considerable amount of walking during
retreat. There is still beauty in the image my memory con-
jures up of brothers taking solitary walks slowly through the
lush gardens or lazily down the dusty roads. This was walking for the soul—no calculating of heartbeats, no effort to
get anywhere, no concern for speed, no worry about going
around in circles.

Simply getting away from linear life, going away in
mood or reflection, walking away from the action, or shut-
ting down business as usual: This is all the start of retreat
and the core of the monastic spirit—only a walk away.

*I*N THEIR POVERTY MONKS DO NOT GLO-rify pennilessness and want, but tone down their acquisitiveness and desire for possessions. We could incorporate the monastic experience of common ownership into capitalism. I own the bridge and the waterway, the woods and city hall, the park and the main artery out of town. On the other hand, I don't truly own the land I live on or the car I drive or even the shirt I'm wearing.

Woody Allen tells the story of his uncle who on his deathbed sold his nephew a watch. People who can give gracefully appreciate the mystery that monks have been preaching for centuries: great riches are to be had by those who surrender their possessiveness.

Wealth needs poverty of a kind in order to be complete and fulfilling.

WHEN I WAS LIVING THE VOW OF CELI-
bacy, a man asked me how I got along without sex. "I
don't," I said. He gave me a look I've never forgotten that
said: Ah! Masturbation or a lover in town or *Penthouse*
under the mattress. I was thinking: the pleasure of living
this communal, natural, interior life *is* sexual. I don't feel
anything missing.

We can all take the vow of chastity in the midst of a
vibrant sex life. The beauty of being with one person sexu-
ally is fed by saying no to others, by not giving too much
attention to sexual longing, by sublimating in imagination
without repression, by finding that the world itself is a sex
partner.

Celibacy is a rounding out of sex, just as sex is a natural outcome of chastity. In Botticelli's *Primavera* Chastity
dances with Beauty and Pleasure, not with Sobriety and
Severity.

*I*N MONASTIC LIFE TIME IS NOT MEASURED by a clock. The day may be set out according to the parts of Divine Office, a set of psalms and songs chosen according to the remembrance of the day—a saint, a liturgical season, a holy event. Lauds, prime, terce, sext, none, vespers, and compline are the "hours" of a sacred day.

Qualities of time are also evoked by chants. *Puer Natus* for Christmas, *Victimae Paschali* for Easter, *Dies Irae* for death. I can't listen to the chant of *Te Deum* without feeling the emotional release of ending a long retreat. We all have music that is tied to special times, and is therefore a means for celebrating the seasons of the soul. We could all learn from monks to disregard our watches and find other more imaginative, sacred ways to mark time.

*T*HERE WAS A MAN IN OUR COMMU-
nity who was always prompt, studious, generally serious,
and obviously destined for a role among the hierarchy. He
was a perfect target for monastic humor.

One night he arrived at his room to find life-sized statues
of a male and female saint lying next to each other in his
bed. On another occasion, just to add a spice of humility to
his habit of promptness, some of his more thoughtful con-
freres unscrewed the handles on his door, so that when the
bell for vespers rang, no matter how much he tried, he
couldn't get the door open.

What is the humor within the joke here? Don't saints
sleep together? Don't we know from Pygmalion that statues
have their own private lives? Aren't we always being
locked in when we have important things to do elsewhere?

A PILGRIM WAS WALKING A LONG road when one day he passed what seemed to be a monk sitting in a field. Nearby men were working on a stone building.

"You look like a monk," the pilgrim said.

"I am that," said the monk.

"Who is that working on the abbey?"

"My monks," said the man. "I'm the abbot."

"It's good to see a monastery going up," said the pilgrim.

"They're tearing it down," said the abbot.

"Whatever for?" asked the pilgrim.

"So we can see the sun rise at dawn," said the abbot.

I'M SURE THE DAY MY DOCTOR DECIDED TO visit the monastery he hadn't the slightest thought that the prior would throw him into the swimming pool. He stood with his nobility firmly in place at the beginning of the party, but when his wife was nudged into the water by a clumsy brother passing by, he may have begun to change his mind about what a monastery was.

Superficial solemnity, thankfully, was never part of my experience of the life. I have always favored the kind of spiritual involvement that begets rather than kills earthy humor and even ribaldry. The perspective of divinity can be defined as all that is contrary to human intention and dignified expectation. We know we are moving more deeply into the spirit when we notice the presence in us of holy foolishness. And who is to say that this was not a case of baptismal renewal!

*W*E COULD ALL TAKE THE VOW OF OBE-dience, even as we pursue freedom and individuality. Obedience means to listen closely to others for words of direction. Only in an ego-mad world do we think that destiny is revealed in our own will and thought.

You know something that I don't know about where I want to be. If I just listen to myself, I will be trapped in a circle. If you don't speak to me about what you see and suspect, then I won't know the direction in which I want to go.

And if I don't listen to my friends and neighbors, I'll be stuck in the labyrinth of what I think I want. Obedience is a way of being communal, but if I'm not in community, obedience will become slavery. The monk sees the will of God in his superior. I can see the deep will that guides me in the thoughts and reflections of my neighbor.

I WAS NINETEEN WHEN I SOUGHT SPIRItual guidance from the novice master whose brother was a professional contemplative, though he himself had an attractive mix of earth and sky. He was an amiable, highly cultured man, who as a leader could be warm without being ingratiating. As was the custom, I prostrated myself on the floor in front of him and kissed my scapular when he gave the sign to rise.

"I've been reading a book on meditation," I said, "that claims the best way is to have a conversation with Christ. I'm trying, but it seems that I'm doing all the talking."

"Just keep listening until you hear something," he said. That was all.

Thirty-four years later, not having seen this novice master all that time, out of the blue I received a letter from him and then visited him at his monastery. I found in him the same dry humor, even more culture, and a new degree of gentleness. Maybe because the trappings of authority and student were now absent, I felt a strong love for him and appreciation for what he had given me in my youth.

Now, having read Jung, Ficino, Yeats, Rilke, and Dickinson, I've discovered how to listen meditatively. It has taken me thirty years to learn how to stop talking, to wait and really listen.

The truly extraordinary discovery is knowing that I still have a novice master.

*I*N TWELVE YEARS OF LIVING IN A COMMU-
nity of men I discovered that monks could be heterosexual
and still be attracted to each other. I never witnessed any
acting out of those attractions, but I could sense the passions
and the longings.

A student of theology once told me that whenever she
took a class in her major, she developed an extreme longing
for sex. Could it be that wherever sex is absent—wherever—it shows its displeasure in obsession? Would a sexier
theology course have had a different effect? What if school
were fundamentally sexy? What if we allowed all of life to
be suffused with desire, sensuality, and pleasure?

I imagine the result to be fewer concerns about people's
sexual choices, more interesting sex in the movies, less
moralism and education in matters of sex, and deeper pleasures in ordinary life. We still haven't learned what the
monks knew well: that sex has little to do with biology.

WHEN I WAS TWENTY AND LIVING IN a priory in Ireland, a perceptive and generous old man took me under his tutelage and told me countless stories of great writers and painters he had known. At the time he was a close friend of Samuel Beckett, a writer for whom even then I felt a certain kinship. He and Beckett were planning a vacation in Venice and invited me to accompany them. I rushed to the prior, the head of the monastery, and asked permission to spend two weeks in Italy. He looked at me as though I had asked him to buy me a Jaguar convertible. "Absolutely out of the question," he said with considerable finality.

At the time my imagination allowed me only regret. Rules were rules and priors were priors. Now I think rather differently. I know about Giordano Bruno, for instance, a monk who traveled from one country to the next, teaching outrageous ideas in a place until he was run out. Now I realize I had other options. I could have gone to Venice and then begged for reinstatement, or I could have joined the Jesuits, or I could have embarked on my own European education. This last option gives me pleasure just in the fantasy of it.

In spiritual lifestyles one often loses touch with one's own freedom and imagination.

*D*URING MY LAST YEARS IN A RELIG-
ious community I had a friend who was too worldly for the
authorities. He was an extraordinarily intelligent and tal-
ented man, a true friend, and, though living a thoroughly
secular life, a lover of the monastic traditions. I was told he
couldn't come to see me, and I wasn't to spend time with
him away from the monastery.

The prior was probably afraid I might be led so much
into the delights of a more worldly life that I'd leave my
vows. The prior was right. I did leave my vows, and my
friend was certainly an influence in that direction. Each person played his role: the tempting friend, the protective
authority, and the wide-eyed pilgrim—me.

Nevertheless, destiny and fate have strong hands, and
necessity waits upon no good reason or loyalty. Happy are
we who find authorities inside us and outside, who can do
their job of protection and guidance, while at the same time
lighting a votive at the altar of necessity.

*T*HE GREATEST BLESSING TO ME OF LIVing for twelve years in a religious community was the opportunity to meet many extraordinary individuals. From the outside, people look at monks and see habits and cowls. From the inside you see souls.

The composer Monteverdi said there are three passions: love, hate, and prayer. All three were in play in the religious community. More interesting is how prayer fosters both solitude and love. Men who pray together several hours each day, and then work, play, and think hard, enjoy a special kind of communal connection.

There is little room for sentimentality, but if the idealism of the praying seeps down into emotions of genuine intimacy, a rare strain of conviviality comes into being, and there is nothing more fulfilling.

Today prayer seems to be largely out of vogue, and so, coincidentally, is conviviality.

*O*NCE, IN THE EARLY YEARS OF MY MON-
astic life, a young man was visiting who said he had a date
that night and needed a haircut. He noticed our barbershop,
which looked quite professional, but what he didn't know
is that in religious community it's the custom for each monk
to take a new job every six months. The "barber" had just
begun his stint, and the young man went away that day
with a hat pulled down over his inexpertly thatched head.

I developed appendicitis on a soccer field in Ireland and
went to the "infirmarian" to get some advice. We all tended
to believe that in our various offices we knew what we
were doing. He recommended hot compresses. When the
doctor arrived to take me to the hospital for surgery, he recommended cold compresses. Definitely nothing warm, he
said.

All of this suggests that we can survive without experts,
and maybe even discover community in the common dis-
pensing of offices.

A BILLBOARD NEAR AN OLD HOUSE OF mine displayed in six-foot type: PRAY. IT WORKS. I always thought this was the ultimate in American pragmatism. If it doesn't work, do you stop praying? What does it mean to say that prayer works? You get what you want? Life gets better?

My billboard would say: PRAY. IT MAY NOT WORK. Prayer is an alternative to working hard to get what you want. One discovers eventually that what you want is almost always what you don't need.

Pray—period! Don't expect anything. Or better, expect nothing. Prayer cleanses us of expectations and allows holy will, providence, and life itself an entry. What could be more worth the effort—or the noneffort?

*I*N THE MONASTERY OUR CUSTOM WAS TO wear a habit, or you could say, our habit was to wear a costume. I wore black for twelve years: a long tunic, thick belt, narrow band down front and back (scapular), and cowl. Attached to the belt was a rosary—beads, seven times seven, counting the sorrows that Mary endured as mother of Jesus.

Marsilio Ficino, my Italian Renaissance guide in matters of magic, taught that one should wear colors for their spiritual effect rather than randomly or according to momentary taste. Certain colors attract a certain kind of spirit.

What did my black habit attract all those years? Certainly a degree of sobriety. An Englishman once noticed a group of us dressed in black and asked: "What are you? You look rather grim."

But black also evokes eternity, as in black holes, and withdrawal, as in black moods. Whatever the mood, making a habit out of a costume serves retreat from the world.

*T*HE MAJOR PART OF A MONK'S LIFE IS given to a strange "work"—liturgy. The word means "public work or performance." We laypersons think of work as something we do to make a living and stay alive, care for our families, find meaning, and achieve a modicum of success. We may justify our lives by it.

The monk gives up this source of meaning and transfers it to "soul work." The work of the monk is liturgy.

We could discover from the example of the monk that there is a place for an odd kind of work that feeds the soul but not necessarily the body. A few moments with a painting, a sunset, a sonata, nothing—might give the soul its sustenance, its meaning, and its reason for existence.

*W*HAT IS THE PROBLEM WITH CONSUMERISM? It's not in shopping, buying, having, owning, selling, enjoying. All these are ways of being attached to the world of objects—not a bad thing in itself. The problem is that in shopping, buying, and possessing we are never satisfied, and that the feeling of emptiness after such an effort to possess indicates that for all our buying we never fully possess or fully own.

I suspect that the soul needs to have and to own, and these needs are perhaps the shadow of spiritual self-denial. The monk's vow of poverty may have nothing to do with this moralistic denial of pleasure.

What does it take to really own and possess? It means loving a thing so much that one can't be parted from it, can't stand to see it neglected and misused, can't trust that someone else will care for it sufficiently.

Our materialism is a sign that we don't love the world nearly enough.

$\mathcal{F}$OR REASONS I HAVE NEVER UNDER-
stood, our community once moved from a much loved,
beautiful, warmly furnished monastery to the cold wing of
a nearby diocesan seminary. We looked at the colorless ter-
razzo floors and pale, plain walls of our new abode and
made it our first order of business to bring in lamps, paint-
ings, paint, soft couches, and comfortable chairs. Within a
few months we began getting requests from local seminari-
ans to join our community.

Oddly it was the worldliness and body sense of us
monks that seemed to attract the so-called secular priests-to-
be. When spirituality and worldliness are so infused with
each other that it is difficult to distinguish one from the
other, they are both brimming with soul and become
objects of desire.

*I*T IS SAID THAT PRIESTS AND MONKS ONCE practiced the rule of *jus primae noctis*, the right of the first night. The clergyman would celebrate the wedding of a couple and then spend the first night with the bride. A four-teenth-century priest had a long affair with a woman whose wedding he had performed. Her husband said, "With the priest it's all right, but stay away from other men."

The monk lives according to the advice of Marsilio Ficino — partly in time, partly in eternity. Whatever is done is never fully of this world, and yet it's always in this world. We could all live partly out of this world, and perhaps discover the limits of worldly law and convention.

God himself is born!
And so we see, God is not
until he is born.

And also we see
there is no end to the birth of God.

D. H. Lawrence

AN INTELLIGENT, KIND MAN LIVED IN
our community for many years, and I admired him greatly.
The prior, however, was constantly annoyed by this man's
independent thinking and gave him grief on every occasion. I'm not one to stand up quickly or forcefully, but this
time I couldn't watch the injustice quietly. I told the prior
that I was quite disturbed at the way he was treating this
valuable member of the community.

The next week my friend was asked unceremoniously
and authoritatively to leave the community that loved him
and of which he had been part for at least six years. He was
told that his manner was a serious disturbance to the others.
Several months later a small revolution took place in the
politics of the order, and the prior lost his position.

I have no doubt about the necessity and fatefulness of my
friend's leave-taking, but I learned through strong emotions
that spiritual authority can easily lose one of the soul's greatest gifts—conscience. Righteousness can be a form of in-
sanity in which conscience, protector of community, is
swamped and undone by entitlement.

$\mathcal{M}$Y MEMORY OF MONASTIC LIFE IS
filled with comedy—practical jokes, elaborate stories, improbable personalities, the great stand-up comic monks, the lore and legends of grand foolishness. On solemn occasions the humor seemed to be especially intense—a cracked voice during a solemn chant, miscues in ritual, food spilling during silent meals, vestments accidentally put on backward.

Then there is the spirit that seems deprived of the capacity for laughter. It can be so severe, sincere, and focused that humor appears alien and almost criminal.

Humor lubricates and softens the spiritual life, and makes it bearable.

A YOUNG WOMAN WHOSE FAMILY was living in poverty tried hard to enter a more promising world by getting her high school diploma, but the state had decided that all students should pass difficult math tests, which she had failed. "We must raise our standards," said the superintendent of schools. "We must be able to compete in the next century. The Chinese and Japanese know their math," he said, "and so should we all."

When educators lose their compassion to principle, to ambition, and to competition, soul has once more been pulverized by a misplaced desire for success. When the individuality of the person is subjugated to general principles of the whole, the soul begins to fade. Principle, futurity, and totalitarianism take over.

The most difficult lesson to learn about caring for the soul is that our best and most cherished ambitions are its worst enemy.

*I*N THE BEST OF MONASTERIES THE PURSUIT of beauty and spiritual practice go hand in hand. Music, architecture, decoration, language, gardens, and libraries flourish. Community life is the object of central concern. Learning, study, reading, and the preservation of books are all integral to spiritual practice.

We get into trouble in the spirit when we give up any of these: when beauty turns into sentimentality or propaganda, when architecture and the other arts are unconscious or considered secondary, when we forget the importance of ongoing, lifelong learning in all areas as support for the spiritual life, and especially when we make spiritual practice the project of creating a certain kind of self.

I'VE NEVER HAD THE IMPRESSION THAT Jesus or the Buddha were proselytizers. It simply wasn't their style to run membership campaigns or even to "network." They seem to have been less ambitious than that.

Believers and followers and converts—words we use of those who have become convinced of some spiritual value—run the risk of trying to make everyone else as perfect as they are. You must read this book, listen to this speaker, go to this place, become a whatever. What is it when the spirit gets such a hold on a person that they have to convert everyone else to their enthusiasm!

Soul puts reins on this tendency to clone one's own tongues of fire. Soul respects another's failure to find perfection, resistance to enlightenment, sheer ignorance of absolute truth, misguided attachments, and unrelenting meandering.

Old pond,
frog jumps
Plop.

*T*HE SOUND OF WATER IN BASHŌ'S POEM about the frog has been translated in a variety of ways— splash, shhh, plop. Good sounds can't easily be put into ordinary words.

One day I'd like to open my own musical instrument store in which I would sell fountains of running water tuned in fourths and fifths, and trees with leaves voiced for sleep that could be placed near a bedroom window, and long metal tubes of such low resonance they could be felt but not heard, and beehives in which the pedal point of the bees could be amplified with a sounding box, and treble frogs and bass frogs, and stones that could be dropped on each other for percussion, and drinking glasses that could be either struck lightly or rubbed, and a bird feeder that would attract a variety of singers, and fish that would make sonorous bubbles in a pond.

My store would be called Bashō's Pond.

*W*HY IS IT SO DIFFICULT FOR A RICH PERson to find heaven that it would be easier for a camel to pass through the eye of a needle? Granted the needle's eye may be a metaphor, the image is nevertheless striking. Which end of the camel would go first, if he gave it a try at all?

Is it that the pursuit of money for power, prestige, and comfort is so far removed from the concerns of the spirit? I don't think it's how much money you have, but rather how much of yourself you give to it. A person with money may not be rich in the biblical sense, and a person with modest quantities may be distracted by its weight.

According to an old Irish story, a monk had a prized possession, a fly that walked along each line of his breviary as he read the psalms. One day the fly died, and the monk lamented the loss to his spiritual director. His friend's admonishing reply: "Misfortune always waits upon wealth."

*S*T. THOMAS MORE WROTE IN *UTOPIA*: What you cannot turn to good you must make as little bad as you can.

He lived a vibrant family life, enjoyed political power, and always sought the monastic spirit. A man for all seasons, his life was a zodiac of attachments and devotedness. In particular he followed an ancient humanist insight: the life of the spirit flourishes in combination with a subtle, reserved, carefully focused life of pleasure.

If you aim at a life of spiritual purity, then you, more than most, must cultivate honest worldly pleasures.

*I*S IT OBLIVION OR ABSORPTION, EMILY Dickinson asks, when we forget?

When some new thought, feeling, or notion presents itself, we can't forget it or overlook it. When we have invited it in or agreed to live in its company, maybe then it won't be such a preoccupation. It will be forgotten—not exiled into oblivion, but absorbed into being.

*I*T IS SAID THAT MICHELANGELO COULD SEE the sculpture in a raw piece of marble. Could it also be a talent to see the marble out of which our things are born?

We tend to look at all the things of life, from objects to people, as fixed, separate, one-dimensional givens. Could we also perceive the stories in which they live, the spirit that gives them context, the music made by their movements, the aromas emanating from their presence, the void displaced by their forms, the secrets hidden by their revelation? What kind of senses would be required for such perception?

*M*ARSYAS, A FIGURE IN MYTHOLOGY
who played the flute or oboe, challenged Apollo to a con-
test. The muses judged the competition, and Marsyas lost,
his punishment the flaying of his skin.

The torture of the mortal by the god who inspires him
was a central theme in the revival of ancient mysteries, says
art historian Edgar Wind of Renaissance sacred art. The
mythological flaying of Marsyas was a prime image of this
mystery that may be implicated in all serious experiments in
the spiritual life. Our small, protective intentions in spirituality, sustained sometimes by sentimentalities, may be
chewed to pieces, their skin ripped off, and their insides
turned out, as we discover the awesome nature of what we
innocently name divine and angelic.

*O*RPHEUS AND EURYDICE. ORPHIC DARK
underworld spirituality is as sacred and close to divinity as
any sky, mountain, light-centered quest for spirit. But the
mystery of Orpheus confounds with its antipathetic logic. If
you want to retrieve from the depths your treasure, that
which you love, indeed your own soul, in that eternal
moment between life and deathly oblivion you must not
look at it. The very goal of spiritual quest disappears instant-
ly when it is perceived.

So, generation after generation the Orphic poets speak of
that which they have never seen and will never see as long
as they are in its presence.

*A*S MONKS SING THEIR CHANTS THEY are making music that mirrors and models the life they are living. Chant is modal. It doesn't have the drive toward ending or the insistent relationships between notes and chords that modern music has. Endings and climaxes appear melodically, for the most part, with a felt lift in song and a sure entropy in musical energy.

A modal life reflecting the chant would be created more by art than by plain emotion. It would be individual (melodic) rather than collective (harmonic). In a modal life, endings are soft, peaks are rounded, and energy is reserved. Modal life, like modal music, has the special beauty that comes with the absence of drivenness.

I've never seen monks waltz, and I'm not sure that their lives rock and roll.

*B*ECAUSE THE LIFE OF A MONK IS ESSEN-
tially a withdrawal from the world, it's necessary for the
monk almost every day to say no to some invitation from
modern life. Monasteries are often difficult to approach
physically. They may have long entrance drives, stout gates
and fences, heavy doors, loud bells, a labyrinth of corridors,
and notices in Latin. These are ritual forms hinting at a cru-
cial spirit that resists modern culture.

If we want to don the metaphoric costume of the monk
in our quest for spirituality, we might learn this art of indi-
rection and concealment, ultimately a means for preserving
one's own spiritual integrity. The world should have a difficult time gaining entrance.

IN A JAPANESE STORY A RENOWNED teacher of archery goes to a mountaintop to find the greatest archer in the world. He's astonished to discover that this accomplished master doesn't use a bow and arrow. Yet, when the master aims his empty arms, formed as though to shoot, into the sky, and then releases the invisible arrow, a bird falls to the earth.

What I envision is a rebuilding of monasticism without the need for monasteries, a recovery of sacred language without a church in which to use it, an education in the soul that takes place outside of school, the creation of an artful world accomplished by persons who are not artists, the emergence of a psychological sensibility once the discipline of psychology has been forgotten, a life of intense community with no organization to belong to, and achieving a life of soul without having made any progress toward it.

*S*OME RENAISSANCE THEOLOGIANS worked hard at reconciling paganism with Judaism and Christianity. We have yet to achieve this detente that is essential to the life of soul. Fragments of our hearts and minds are located in the garden of Gethsemane and in the garden of Epicurus, on the zodiac of the Apostles and on the zodiac of the animals, in the wine of Dionysus and in the wine of the Eucharist, in the psalms of David and in the hymns of Homer.

It is not a matter of belonging to a religion or professing one's faith, it is a matter of orientation in life and participation in its mysteries. We can all be pagan in our affirmation of all of life, Christian in our affirmation of communal love, Jewish in our affirmation of the sacredness of family, Buddhist in our affirmation of emptiness, and Taoist in our affirmation of paradox.

The new monk wears invisible robes. Thomas Merton travels across the globe, and in the home of Eastern monks, dies. Isn't this a myth for our time about the resurrection of the monastic spirit!

*S*T. COMPASSUS AND HIS BAND OF EIGHT
monks lived for years in a land-locked region of forests and
valleys. One day the saint rose in the morning with the
thought that he and his men were destined to find a new
land across the sea. He had the advantage of both book
learning and a certain intuitive, divinitory form of knowledge, and so every day for five years he read about the sea
and about unknown lands. At the same time he consulted
the flight of migrating birds and the shape of clouds and the
peal of thunder.

When all was set, the small band climbed into the
homemade craft they had brought to the ocean's shore, and
amid jeers from their countrymen who believed the land-
lubber crew would perish in the unfamiliar sea, they set off
from the rocky edge of land. St. Compassus knew exactly
where the craft should head, but a current turned them
around in the first minute of their voyage, and they sailed
away, first in circles, then in a serpentine squiggle, and
finally straight ahead in the wrong direction. They were
never heard from again.

*O*NE DAY, WHEN THE MONK IS AB-
sorbed into the life of culture, theology will also have been
restored and revisioned. It will be a rich study of religions
and nonreligions, philosophies and poetries, fictions and
musics, beliefs and unbeliefs.

In my daydreams this new theology takes her place
alongside the arts and sciences, and her objects of study
include culture's daily diet of ritual, prayer, icon, ceremony,
architecture, holy reckoning of time, illness, death, birth,
marriage, yearning, melancholy, meaning, lack of meaning, history, ancestors, values, morality, atonement, and
initiation.

One day, instead of going to a therapist, troubled or
searching people will pay a call on their theologian to consider the mysteries that have befallen them.

*S*OMETIMES IN THEIR CHANTING MONKS will land upon a note and sing it in florid fashion, one syllable of text for fifty notes of chant. Melisma, they call it.

Living a melismatic life in imitation of plainchant, we may stop on an experience, a place, a person, or a memory and rhapsodize in imagination. Some like to meditate or contemplate melismatically, while others prefer to draw, build, paint, or dance whatever their eye has fallen upon.

Living one point after another is one form of experience, and it can be emphatically productive. But stopping for melisma gives the soul its reason for being.

*M*ATINS. THE MORNING PRAYER OF the monastery, named after Matuta, Goddess of Dawn, according to Lucretius. For years I rose at 5:15 A.M. to a knock at my door and a Latin greeting from a confrere. "*Ave Maria*," Hail Mary, he would say in a muffled voice on the other side of the door, breaking into my dreams. "*Gratia Plena*," Full of Grace, was my reply, although it was often said with more growl than grace.

It is of the essence of the monk's life to rise early. Whenever we get up in the small hours of morning we participate in the monk's praise and enjoyment of dawn. In this liminal place, on the threshold between dream and life, sleep and waking, and darkness and sunshine, we find a special doorway to the spiritual and the eternal.

The monk seeks out periods of spiritual ripeness and simply opens his heart to their effluence.

*T*HE MONK'S LIFE OF CHASTITY IS LIVED to a full degree as a life station, but chastity is available to us all, single or married, as one positive element among many. Being chaste, we need not give all our thoughts and time to the pursuit of sex, which is not fulfilled in such singleminded devotion anyway. In chastity we reserve a good part of ourselves for relation to others—to people, places, and things, and we have the conviction to be individual, solitary, and self-contained.

The soul enjoys sensations of purity, as long as they are not bought at the price of impurity's delights.

The monk has to find his lay soul, just as the layperson searches for the monk soul.

Purity, sometimes achieved by the ritual washing of hands, has long been celebrated as a needed preparation for the incursion of spirit. Such chastity may last no longer than a fleeting moment and yet satisfy the requirements for a spiritual grace.

*A*S MONKS, WE DIDN'T DINE, WE RE-
fected. We never used that word, but the room in which we
ate, the long hall with tables set on the outer sides only, we
called the refectory. The word refers to being remade or
refreshed at a meal. Nonmonks use a similar word, restaurant, which means to be restored.

Still, the refectory had its own style of dining and its
own method of restoration. Most days we ate in silence. I
wonder if the silence that sometimes descends upon people
at a restaurant is due to a passing monkish spirit and not to
a failure of communication.

Often a brother would read a thoughtful book aloud
while the rest of us ate—being restored in mind as well as
body. Certain restaurants—delis, coffee shops, bakeries—
seem suited for reading while eating, thus keeping refection
alive. Thought for food.

*T*HREE MONKS KNELT IN THE CHAPEL IN the dark morning hours before dawn.

The first thought he saw the figure of Jesus come down from the cross and rest before him in midair. Finally, he said to himself, I know what contemplation is.

The second felt himself rise out of his place in the choir. He soared over his brother monks and surveyed the timber-vaulted ceiling of the church, and then landed back in his place in the choir. I've been blessed, he thought, with a minor miracle, but in humility I must keep it to myself.

The third felt his knees growing sore and his legs tired. His mind wandered until it came to a stop on the image of a luscious hamburger laden with onions and pickles.

"No matter how hard I try," said the devil's helper to his master, "I can't seem to tempt this third monk."

*T*HE ARTS GIVE THE SPIRITUAL LIFE IMAG-
nation, softening its tendency toward rules and dogma and
deepening its intuitions. Monastic architecture, so unique
and so deeply moving, is of the essence of that spiritual life,
in no way secondary.

Every home is a monastery. There, it is to be hoped, we
can find solitude, community, beauty, nature, oratory, and
food. There the spirit can be nourished, and the body
pleased with arts and pleasures.

When planning a home, a remodeling, or a new
arrangement of furniture, we could do worse than study the
plans and pictures of a great monastery of the past.

*T*HE MONK'S LIFE MAY APPEAR TO BE extraordinary, but in truth it is exceptional for being so utterly ordinary.

For years I conducted my fellow brothers in Gregorian chant. The chant may sound simple, but it required daily evening rehearsals. We didn't have an expert choir chosen by audition, we had a choir of men who happened to live in a particular monastery. A few were downright tone-deaf. Some were basses whose pitch hovered above and below the appointed note. Others were tenors whose voices tended to crack and gargle at a certain high range. Each had a different idea about how long it should take to reach the end of the piece.

But we sang beautiful chant, and therein is a lesson about making something extraordinary out of less than ordinary talents.

*T*HE MONK PRACTICES SPIRITUAL READ-
ing. For him, a book is not a source of information, but a
way to pray. What if we always read as prayer, every book
a scripture, whether science, fiction, or theology! Our
minds might release some of their authority and influence,
allowing our hearts, or some other place of reflection, to be
nourished.

Monks also spoke of the world as a book, *liber mundi.*
How do you study the world without trying to be informed! The answer to that question defines the difference
between the religious and the secular life.

$\mathcal{W}$HAT I PARTICULARLY LIKE ABOUT the image of the monk is that he is always out of place. A picture stays in my mind of a priest in our community who was extraordinarily bright and also very funny. He had a bad back and often had to use a heating pad. One day as we were chanting vespers I looked over to the opposite choir stall and saw him standing there with a cord trailing from somewhere in his habit to an outlet in the wall. The electric monk.

The incongruousness of a plugged-in monk or a nun at a bank ATM machine says something about the religious life. It is always an anachronism, because eternal time is always somewhat out of synch with ordinary calendar time. This also suggests that whenever we feel that we belong in another century or we can't seem to keep up with the pace of modern life, the monk may be paying a visit, and his spirit could be cultivated rather than cured.

*I*N HIS RECOLLECTIONS OF THOMAS MER-
ton, before talking about their common approach to world
peace, the Dalai Lama noted that he learned from Merton
to wear a thick belt instead of a thin cord around his waist.
Imagine the Dalai Lama and Merton in deep conversation
comparing Buddhist notions of compassion with Christian
ideas of charity, the great religious leader all the time eyeing
the monk's belt with some envy, and then later copying the
monk's ways.

Here we have an extraordinary example of religious
learning — imitating the holy figure we admire — as well as
living in the stereoscopic world in which one eye is on the
cosmos and the other on a belt, a perfect reconciliation of
time and eternity.

*P*LANS FOR MONASTERIES ALWAYS CALL
for a chapel. In the life of the monk, spiritual practice is central—liturgy, meditation, divine office, prayer—and so the
room dedicated to this work is an important part of the
architecture.

Any of our buildings—houses, civic centers, office
plazas, shopping malls, places of industry—could also rec-
ognize that spirituality is a central element of life. Each
could have a chapel, if only a simple room, dedicated exclu-
sively to the needs of the soul.

What shift in attitude would be required should our
architects consider a chapel as an absolute necessity in any
building project?

IN THE TWELFTH CENTURY JOACHIM OF
Fiore created a sensation with his theology or philosophy of
time. There is an age of the Father, the Son, and the Holy
Spirit, he said, of law, grace, and spirit. As I read Joachim, I
imagine three phases in each person's life and in the history
of a culture. There is a time to focus on law, learning, and
guidance. Later, one discovers structures that serve one's
needs—church, a school of thought, marriage. Finally, one
finds all of these things sublimated—less literal, concrete
but not obvious.

I prefer the intention to be in community over intentional communities. We nonmonks may think of community involvement as something added on to our private
lives. The monk knows that the individual fulfillment he
craves can only be found in perpetual attention to community.

$\mathcal{B}$ROTHER PHILIP WAS BAKING BREAD in the kitchen, as he had done most of his life as a brother and a baker. The day before, his spiritual director had advised him, when discussing Brother Philip's inclination toward anger, especially at his fellow monks, to think dark thoughts as he kneaded the bread and then bake them in the holy fires of the furnace oven.

So Brother Philip happily conjured all the bile his memory preserved and fingered it forcefully into the tawny dough. He kneaded, fingered, remembered, and kneaded again. He set the dough aside to rise in a warm place, and then returned later to punch it down with unusual force. Finally, he placed the much worked dough into the oven and slept the first restful nap he had taken in years.

In the great oven the loaf began to rise. It rose and rose. A passerby wondered why the monastery windows appeared to be covered with oat-colored curtains. By day's end the monastery was engulfed by the bread. As time passed the dough hardened to petrification, and much later another generation of monks stood at the base of the mountain chanting: "You are Peter, and upon this rock I will build my church."

$\mathcal{F}$OR THE MONK WORK IS PRAYER, READing is contemplation, following orders is listening to the word of God, community is a foretaste of heaven, time is at least 50 percent determined by ritual, and celibacy is a positive prerequisite for service in the world. Ordinary details of life are always imagined through a filter of sacredness.

The secularization of modern sensibility is so unconscious that it may seem odd to consider a similar sacrilization for us all. Yet, without imagination for the sacred in everyday experience, we are destined for a life without soul. The two—soul and the sacred—go together. We don't have to become monks, but we can learn from their example how to bring the monastic spirit, as a color and a flavor, into modern life.

*T*HE LIFE OF THE MONK SEEN THROUGH
sentimental eyes can be easily misunderstood. It's a tough
life, in which sensitivity to interior thoughts and feelings
are intense, and a similar attention to the presence of others
in the community makes relationship particularly challeng-
ing. In modern life it may appear that real work is located in
the heroics of surviving and succeeding in the world. For
the monk the challenge is in nonheroic intimacy with oneself, others, and the world.

The monk's occupation is soul work. In religious community I was always told that the mere presence of a priory
in a neighborhood was a contribution to the area. If we do
not have monks in our midst, we might not know of this
soul-centered approach to life that the monks model, teach,
and demonstrate. Our task is to discover in the monks how
to bring soul closer to the center of a generally secular life
and make the switch from heroics to intimacy.

AN IMPORTANT PART OF THE LIFE OF many monks is study. In a stereotypical image, the monk is reading in silence in a library. Historians associate monasticism with reading, writing, and publishing. Like everything else in modern life, learning is generally considered a secular pursuit, but the monks show us that study can be a spiritual practice.

We study to get diplomas and degrees and certifications, but imagine a life devoted to study for no other purpose than to be educated. Being educated is not the same as being informed or trained. Education is an "eduction," a drawing out of one's own genius, nature, and heart. The manifestation of one's essence, the unfolding of one's capacities, the revelation of one's heretofore hidden possibilities—these are the goals of study from the point of view of the person. From another side, study amplifies the speech and song of the world so that it's more palpably present.

Education in soul leads to the enchantment of the world and the attunement of self.

*O*NE OF MY MOST CHERISHED POST-monastery monastic experiences was walking in procession at a service of the Cathedral of St. John the Divine with Dean Morton at my side, on my way to give a Sunday sermon. I was reminded then of many processions during my years in a priory.

Procession is a form of walking, ritual walking. We would process formally into the chapel for special ritual occasions, or into the refectory for special dining occasions, and once a year, during Rogation Days, through fields and gardens, chanting litanies, to bless all the growing things.

Procession is an identifying act of the monk, but it, too, has its counterparts outside the monastery. A family may process into the dining room on a holiday or special occasion. In good restaurants you will be led to your table by a guardian who leads the procession to the table. A procession invites the spirits of the occasion to be present, and it renders the place of gathering the hopeful goal of labyrinthine mystery.

*M*ONKS SPEND A GOOD MEASURE OF their time in meditation. Meditation offers innumerable ways to leave the here and now for the forever. This kind of meditating may last only seconds—as you glimpse a woodpecker climbing up a tree outside your window.

The perceptive religion scholar, Karl Kerényi, describes religious festival as an "arresting." Whatever arrests us invites us to meditation. I am arrested as I play a Bach partita on the piano, or when I come across a Lucas Cranach painting of Venus, or when I stand on a wet beach with a camera in hand, or when I'm inviting the muse to give me a line to write.

I wonder if being arrested by the police has a relation to this religious meditation, and if the monk and the trespasser have something in common.

*W*HENEVER I SEE AN AGED PRIEST OR brother I knew in his youth or midlife, I'm struck by the sense that this person, though now old, is living the same life he lived thirty years ago. Outside the monastery people go through significant external changes. They succeed or they fail. They do things that give them a clear history, while the monk appears to live in an eternal present.

It's as though the timeless soul experience of the monk pours out onto his life and person, while most of us show only the metamorphoses of time.

PRAYER IS A SCANNING OF THE HEAVens for the chink through which angels travel and divinity looks on, like the opening in the dome of the Pantheon in Rome, or on the head of the Hopi in prayer, or the clear sight of the sky in a grove of tall trees, or the fontanelle of a baby.

Or, in the other direction, it's Dante finding an entrance in the woods to the inferno, or the tomb of Jesus, or the place of Orpheus's musical descent, or the Frogs of Aristophanes chanting their Underworld mantra.

Sometimes it's a foxhole, in actual war or in the more ordinary life battles. It might be rimmed with hopelessness or marked out with fear or set with ignorance and chance. Cancer opens the way to prayer, a black hole through which divinity peers and the human discovers infinity.

$\mathcal{T}$HE ROMAN ARCH, SO MUCH A PART
of our image of the monk, preserves eternity. Without it we
ordinary folk daily walk through portals that are flat on top
and bottom. The monk, in contrast, is ever passing through
the earth and sky, the latter the ever-present dome under
which we all live. The monastery is microcosm, the arch a
two-dimensional dome, the dome a constant signal of the
heavens.

Modern life has lost its sense of the dome, thinking
instead, very unmonklike, that the sky reaches out into deep
space. To counter that void of empty space, which has a corresponding effect of hollowing the things of earth, we
would have to reconstruct the dome in imagination. We
would have to restore the monk's vision and corresponding
architecture.

*T*HE MONK'S RELATIONSHIP WITH NA-
ture is essential to the life, but this relationship is not sentimental. It is not basically aesthetic, not environmental, not
naturalist, not agricultural. The monk knows that without a
constant and intimate relationship with nature, divinity is
not fully revealed.

The monastery at the edge of the sea or at the top of
a mountain or on an expanse of farmland is proximate to
nature as revelation. Without knowing nature we cannot
know who we are or what we are to do. Nature shapes us
as much as we shape nature, and in that mutual engagement is the fulfillment of both.

As each year of technological change comes and goes, it
seems that nature loses its influence over the shaping of
human life. It still manifests its power for beauty and for
devastation, but the human response seems to be an in-
creasingly defensive and offensive struggle.

The monk struggles, too, yet has a means of rapproche-
ment in a theology of creation, in prayer, and in worship, all
worked out in day-by-day toil in the earth.

*I*N A MONASTERY LIBRARY I ONCE FOUND
the volume *Opera Platonis* in the music section. The librarian was either unschooled in Latin or perhaps familiar with Plato's *Timaeus* and the music of the spheres.

Many medieval philosophers taught that life is essentially musical, and that it takes a true musical sensibility to reflect philosophically on the nature of things. To the musical philosopher beauty is more convincing than truth, movement more central to life structures than static forms, song more expressive than syllogism, and being moved by a thing's presence more significant than understanding it.

Angels are the only musicians who can play this music, and monks are the only ones who can hear it.

*W*HENEVER I THINK OF A MONK TO-day, I don't think of a Catholic monk or a Christian monk or a Buddhist monk or a Zen monk, and I don't think of male or female monks. I imagine the monk as a spirit that engendered monasticism and moves a certain few individuals to live that spirit as a way of life. For me, the more interesting monk is a figure of the deep, creative imagination, who can inspire anyone toward an experience of virtues and styles epitomized by monks of all traditions.

Our task is to notice the monk when his spirit makes an appearance, and then find an individual way to embody it.

SILENCE IS NOT THE ABSENCE OF SOUND. That would be to imagine it negatively. Silence is a toning down of inner and outer static, noise that occupies not only the ears but also the attention. Silence allows many sounds to reach awareness that otherwise would go unheard—the sounds of birds, water, wind, trees, frogs, insects, and chipmunks, as well as conscience, daydreams, intuitions, inhibitions, and wishes.

One cultivates silence not by forcing the ears not to hear, but by turning up the volume on the music of the world and the soul.

*A*LL THE CLASSICAL THINGS THAT have been said about prayer are true—petition, praise, adoration, communion, conversation. But one's notion of God and divinity has to be sufficiently empty, its mystery sufficiently accounted for, or else prayer becomes exploitation of the divine.

Prayer only makes sense in the paradoxical presence of both human pain and desire on one hand, and divine infinitude on the other.

*A*S EVERYONE KNOWS, THE CATHE-
dral of St. Regianus had a magical rose window that on a
certain day would cast a beam of light down upon a stone
in the pavement of the cathedral's nave, a beam so bright,
warm, and powerful that it was believed to cure illnesses
caused by any dark factors whether inner or outer—a black
mood, a dark enemy, a shadowy infestation, or a cloudy
disposition.

One weekday afternoon, when no one was in the
church, the sacristan brought his cleaning bucket to the reflecting stone, applied a detergent of extraordinary strength,
then an oil used only for the most sacred objects, and finally
a choice piece of chamois for polishing. As the stone lost its
residue of dust and grime, and then when it found its shine
from the soft chamois, the sacristan felt a tingle in his arm.
He looked down and watched his forearm glow with an
otherworldly sheen, and then his forearm withered.

The bishop called for an audience with the sacristan.
"Tell me," said the bishop authoritatively, "is this a miracle!"

"The stone is supposed to heal, not harm," said the sacristan meekly. "I wouldn't call this a miracle."

After this event the authorities allowed the stone to
gather grime and the window to lose its translucence, wor-
ried about the easy transition in such arcane matters from
miracle to maim.

*M*Y MONASTERY HAD A PRACTICE
called "culpa," fault. The friars would gather in the chapel,
the prior sitting in front of the assembly, and certain select
ones from the priests, brothers, and students would approach, prostrate flat on the ground, kiss the scapular, and
rise to tell of a fault, some action that might have offended
the community.

This impulse toward confession is an essential part of
the spiritual life, which, I believe, mitigates rather than
feeds the tendency toward masochistic self-reproach and
sensations of victimization. Confession is an evocation of
remorse, a feeling placed in the heart much deeper than
regret, that keeps the soul intact, neither unconcerned about
its destructive inclinations nor subdued by self-judgment.

*I*S THERE A RELATIONSHIP BETWEEN THE priest who drinks wine in ritual and the person who can't stop drinking in the bar? Both are fascinated by alcohol, and both are drawn into its mystery. The holiness of ritual wine doesn't keep priests from alcoholism, and heavy drinking doesn't lead the alcoholic to sacred mystery.

Still, it is a question whether one needs the other—the priest in need of the alcohol of life, what the Greeks called Dionysus, and the alcoholic in need of the profound fulfillment of his thirst.

*T*HE COWL I WORE AS PART OF MY habit was not intended to keep my ears warm, nor was it merely a vestige of clothing commonly worn at the time of monasticism's flourishing. Rather, it was a ritual covering of my head, a small form of retreat.

Athletes, who are monks in their own way, wear cowls, and cowls are also fashionably attached to capes and sweaters of both men and women. Monasticism still flourishes in sports and in clothing.

The cowl lying ready at the base of our necks prepares us to respond at that moment when the spirit of the monk descends unexpectedly, and asks us to cover our heads in contemplation.

A PARTICULARLY HYPNOTIC FORM OF religious chanted poetry is the litany, often sung by monks on special occasions. *Te rogamus audi nos*, the monks chant, as long lists of saints are sung. Hear us, we beg you.

I think of the many men and women who have touched me during my years and who form a litany of names cherished and feared and fondly remembered. *Te rogamus audi nos*. Hear me, my grandparents, who gave me so much of their hearts. Hear me, friends, who stayed with me in my most unconscious and unripe years. Hear me, my ancestors, whose written words and objects of art have educated me. Hear me, former loves, who feel my rejection and coldness.

Only a finite number of names can be in our litany, and so we sing to them as precious saints who have graced our lives.

$\mathcal{F}$ROM THE OUTSIDE, THE MONASTERY garden can be seen as a romantic, sentimental place of sweet spirituality. From the inside, that garden may be an enclosure of interior torments for the monks who struggle with their desires and passions and self-examinations.

At our homes we can evoke the sweet and the tormented monk in our enclosed gardens, with their trellises and gates, their walking paths and their shade. The soul seems to benefit from having an external manifestation of its internal states. The dialogue between the inner and the outer in this way is the very essence of ritual.

Gardening is a monk's way of caring for the soul.

$\mathcal{M}$ONKS ARE CALLED TO THE "CON-templative" life. The word means to cut out a space for divination. The monk creates an inner temple, a space in mind, imagination, and heart where he can observe the signs of divine providence.

The work of the spiritual life includes the building of these inner temples and the creation of temenos—space set apart for sacred use. As this work progresses, everything acquires its temenos. As Emerson said, everything becomes a sign.

Contemplation, the primary work of the monk, achieves the necessary emptiness in every thing, every moment, and every event. These empty spaces, simply marked out as sacred, invite the soul to participate and provide places for its dwelling.

What birds fly through is not intimate space
in which a form arises.
In the open air you would be dispossessed of yourself
forever.

Space extends out from us and connects to a thing.
To effect the presence of a tree
put innerspace around it
from the pure space that is in you.
Surround it with restraint.
It has no limits.
Only in the containment of your renouncing
will it truly be a tree.

Rainer Maria Rilke

*G*OD IS BEYOND IN THE MIDST OF OUR life, says Bonhoeffer. The monk manages to live this beyond-amid with special gracefulness and beauty. Beauty emerges only when life has achieved radical beyondness while fully amid, or intense amidness by means of beyond.

Oddly, the monk withdraws into the heart of culture and life, into the fullness of community. He withdraws in order to be more involved.

We average persons may need daily withdrawal in order to be more fully participants in community, family, and society. Pull up the cowl, eat in silence, read to be absorbed, pray without intent, chant.

*M*Y COMMUNITY WAS CALLED A mendicant order—begging, living off alms. Today begging is shameful to the middle class, a scandal to those who think everyone can and should work for a living. The homeless person on the street is surrounded by the emotional shadows of reprobation.

Yet, the most spiritual activities are funded by begging: public radio and television, charities, programs for the disadvantaged, medicine, education. Even today many who enter the most meaningful professions become mendicants.

If we are not beggars, we might ask ourselves if we have any spirituality in our lives.

$\mathcal{W}$HAT IS THE DIFFERENCE BETWEEN AN illuminated manuscript created by a monk and a page freshly spewed out of a modern word processor?

The computer page is eminently legible, quickly produced, perhaps beautiful, and created by the collaboration of human and machine. The illuminated page is beautiful, slowly produced, not terribly legible, and printed in solitude. The monk works with his hand, close to his ink, ready for a slip of the pen, meditating as he works.

Is there a way to bring the spirit of the monk to the computer, and by extension to all our machine work, without making either an anachronism?

*T*HE LIBRARY IS OFTEN THE PLACE WHERE you can find the spirit of the monk: in silence, the lustre of old woodwork, the smell of ageing paper, reading, retreat from the world, rules and authorities, tradition, volumes of wisdom, catalogues for contemplation.

In an age of information technology, monks of the library are being put out on the streets, no longer finding a home there. Where will they go?

A home library, if only five volumes on a piece of special wood, might give the monk a place of refuge and serve the souls of all who live there.

A SAINT IS A HOLY PERSON WHOSE LIFE demonstrates how to live fully dedicated to the soul. Some saints are outrageous, some fictitious. Most live so close to the eternal that they are known for performing miracles — actions that are not bound by the limitations of a temporal, merely natural outlook on life.

I've known a few saints in my day, and still enjoy the acquaintance of some. These are not perfect saints, but they have special power due to their intimacy with an angelic dimension. Knowing them is a grace in itself.

Saints are to be sought after, believed in even when they are most incredible, and cherished in memory, story, and devotion.

*I*N A MONASTERY TIME IS CAREFULLY SPENT. Outside, we don't think much of letting one activity lead to another, each taking as much time as needed. But in a monastery there are fifteen minutes for reading, two hours for study, allotted periods for prayer and meditation, usually less than an hour here and there for recreation.

It does no good to think moralistically about how much time we waste. Wasted time is usually good soul time. But there is something especially fruitful in a regulated life, a fantasy of time in which regularity—monasticism is sometimes called the regular life—is not a prison but freedom.

The ritual quality of appointed times releases us from the burdens of free will.

*T*HE DIFFERENCE BETWEEN A TRADI-
tional practice of spirituality and a made-up, "new age" version is immense. Traditional rituals and images rise out of an historical fog in which founders and authorities are more mythological than personal, and in which so many different layers of meaning lie packed together that the sacred literature becomes genuine poetry. This inexhaustible richness is entirely different from one person's intentional program of spiritual progress.

Tradition is often confused with institution, yet we could be guided by countless generations of ancestors without becoming oppressed by the words and structures they have left behind. We could be members of an institution without sacrificing our intelligence or our capacity to think and choose.

Tradition is a pool of imagination, and not a basis for authority.

A RELIGIOUS OR SPIRITUAL AUTHORITY stands in a dangerous position, full of traps. It is in the nature of the spiritual life to think in hierarchies of authority, to imagine meaning in terms of truth, and to invest one person or group of persons with extraordinary influence. Religious leaders require unusual wisdom not to become intoxicated with power and lord it over their followers.

Religious authorities need our own self-governance in spiritual matters. If we "subjects" are making intelligent decisions and educating ourselves, then the leader can offer focus, direction, and structure. But the moment we give too much power to our leaders, we become the victims and they the tormentors. The religious spirit, which needs vibrant external structures, succumbs to empty institutional forms, and rules replace wisdom.

The final belief is to believe in a fiction,
which you know to be a fiction, there
being nothing else. The exquisite truth
is to know that it is a fiction and that
you believe in it willingly.

Wallace Stevens

*S*PIRITUAL COMMUNITIES TAKE SPECIAL note of a person's hair. Some rule against cutting any hair, others make a haircut part of the initiation rite, as in tonsure—the ritual cutting of a monk's hair. Some specify how to curl the hair or to cover it with a turban or kerchief. Some find great spiritual pleasure in shaving the head, others are specific about veils and hats. Television evangelists are sometimes known for their coiffures.

Religion teaches us something extraordinary in this—that hair and its condition is a holy mystery. If hair is sacred, what could possibly not be?

*I*N SPITE OF INTENSE COMMUNITY LIFE, POV-erty, and withdrawal from the world, it is not unusual for monks to travel widely. Thomas Merton, perhaps the most famous monk of our time, who spent many years of his life in a strictly contained monastery, died in Bangkok, halfway across the world from his home monastery.

Monks who travel, like so many spiritual people, have homes in many places. They can stay cheaply in other monasteries or in the homes of people dedicated to the same life. Travel and the hosting of travelers is part of the life, and it shows a typical monastic sublimation of the very idea of home.

Do innkeepers, B & B owners, and hotel managers know of the traditional spiritual nature of their work? Could we all see the monk in people temporarily in search of a place to spend the night? Could we open our hearts as well as our doors to each other as fellow travelers?

*T*HE MONK'S CELIBACY IS NOT SIMPLY the absence of sex and marriage. The monk is not wedded to anything but the infinite, and that relationship is extraordinarily elusive. If you're married to All and Nothing, to the Minimum and the Maximum (in Nicholas of Cusa's wording), you're a celibate in the world.

The monk's life is dedicated to the principle of detachment, but that dedication doesn't mean that he doesn't enjoy and suffer many attachments. A spirit of detachment, celibacy, unweddedness, even amid a plethora of attachments, is exactly that—a spirit, a spirit that doesn't have to dominate in order to influence.

Maybe we ought to be celibate in all that we're wedded to.

*L*IKE MOST MODERN PEOPLE, MONKS have experimented with ways to be both alone and together. Early monasteries were designed so that a monk would live in his own cell and eat from his own garden, and yet participate in a common life with his brothers.

Sometimes people become anxious as they try to live as an individual while in a marriage or other close relationship. Others, who live alone, can be quite anxious about finding a mate or a community.

Monasticism doesn't seem to have been caught up in these anxieties, but rather enjoyed the experiment of living both lives in one place. Maybe our anxiety comes from our attempts to resolve the issue mentally and abstractly. The monk's way is to shape life concretely so that it speaks to both necessities.

A CLOISTER MAY BE PART OF A MONK'S life—a place set apart for utter privacy. The word means partition, and is related to cloisonné, the method in jewelry making of separating sections of stone or enamel with narrow strips of metal. It's striking that a cloister, intended as a way of keeping monks out of the world, is known for its beauty, whether in jewelry or in monasteries.

Cloister is still possible today in the way we build our homes and live our lives. We live in an age of social involvement, when turning in on oneself may appear suspicious. But the monk, dedicated wholeheartedly to community life and to the needs of the world, could be nourished in his soul as he enjoyed the solitude of his comforting cloister.

*S*PIRIT IS THE MOST CREATIVE, INSPIRING, and meaning-giving element in all of life, and yet it is also the most dangerous. When spirit visits us, it moves us toward action, commitment, ambition, goals, ideals, vision, and altruism. All of these feed the soul, but they also wound it. To the soul their opposites are equally important—waiting, doubting, retreating, not going anywhere, not knowing, not seeing, and being absorbed in oneself.

When spirit is not grounded and checked by soul, it quickly moves into literal forms—converting others and becoming blindly and callously ambitious. Its powerful force may turn without conscience into violence, its altruism blackened as intrusion into the freedoms of others. Its creativity becomes unbounded productivity, and its quest for ultimacy transforms into jealous possession of truth.

*W*HEN I WAS A PHILOSOPHY STUDENT in Ireland I had an emergency appendectomy that put me in bed in a hospital ward with twenty other men. It was an active place, that ward—patients raided the kitchen in the middle of the night, distributing forbidden food to those of us who couldn't get out of bed, and many daytime episodes were so funny I thought my stitches would burst in my laughter.

On my first day back at the monastery my Greek professor, a man of intelligence and good humor, accosted me. I suppose you must be far ahead of your classmates in Greek now, he said seriously. In fact, I was at least ten days behind. I had taken the time to live the hospital routine, get to know people, and, of all things, rest. Yet, I felt somewhat guilty, wondering why I couldn't be as disciplined as this revered teacher.

My Greek professor is now dead, but I wonder what he thought late in his life about his drive and discipline. Would he have said, from a lifetime given to spiritual ideals, that he had gone too far, that he might have gained something had he made fewer demands on himself and others? Or was his disciplined life his joy?

*D*URING THE YEAR I LIVED AS A NOVice in the order, a spanking new trainee in religious community life, my brothers and I were not allowed to listen to the radio, leave the grounds, or read newspapers. For a year we were uninformed about world events.

In our time it seems necessary and responsible to know what is happening everywhere in the world. A modern anxiety, perhaps a neurosis, is the need to be informed minute by minute of late-breaking news.

Is the ideal to be found in a balance of these two approaches? Or can we entertain both passions—the adult need to be informed and the childlike need to be unconcerned and irresponsible?

*T*HE DAY ST. CHRISTOPHER, THE SAINT who ferried Jesus across the river on his shoulders, lost his canonization because his historical facticity was seriously questioned, was a bitter day for sacred imagination. The very point of religion is to give utter devotion to images that render life utterly vibrant and meaningful.

Apparently historians and scientists still think that their notions about experience are more fact than fiction, and yet it is abundantly clear, as revision after revision revolutionizes these fields, that at the most fundamental levels and in all fields we live in a grand web of imagination.

The monk has the courage and the folly to shape a life around imagined inspirations.

*A*T CHRISTMAS WE CELEBRATE THE birth of the divine child, or the childhood of divinity, or the divinity of childhood, or the appearance of light and life out of darkness and the fallowness of winter, a child in a manger. It is a mystery that we honor, a mystery that cannot be explained or contained.

This celebration, like all holy rituals, rises out of a particular religious tradition, and yet it is the honoring of a mystery in which all beings, human and otherwise, participate.

The particularity of the monk's life gives it its existence, and yet its unlimited relevance makes it eternally meaningful. The monk's purpose is to shape a life that embraces this paradox of individuality and eternity in every moment and in every act.

*M*OST OF THE MONKS I HAVE MET IN recent years have either been world travelers on their way to Poland, Russia, Israel, or Paris, or they have been caretakers of vast, beautiful expanses of land and buildings that they call home.

Apparently, the spirit of poverty is good soil for the planting of a business and for a life in the global village. Virtues of humility and modesty not only provide purity of heart, they also sharpen a person's commercial talents. Business leaders might be well advised to spend some time in retreat with monks, and learn how to live successfully in this world.

*D*AILY LIFE IN A MONASTERY IS USU-ally punctuated by the ringing of bells. Why are bells associated with churches and monasteries? Perhaps because their overtones are so strong—the high-pitched ringing sounds that decay slowly after the initial clang. In the seventeenth century Robert Fludd depicted angels as the overtones of human life. Joan of Arc loved bells, and said that she heard voices especially when bells were rung for matins and compline, the morning and evening hours of the church day.

Overtones, sometimes called partials by music theorists, are those elements in every experience that last long after the literal act—memories, shock, emotional residues, reactionary behavior. They are also the meanings and implications of deeds, their nuances and reverberation.

Monks are more interested in these partials of experience than in the literal facts. They are professionals in spiritual resonance. When the bell rings, they stop and listen.

*D*URING ONE BUSY YEAR OF MY MON-astic life I had a double major in music and theology. I was taking a difficult course in orchestration when one day my professor assigned me a Beethoven sonata to be arranged for full symphonic orchestra. During that week, after a busy day of monastic routine and classes, I dashed to the piano that was in a large recreation room, tried to remember the ranges of the various instruments, their clefs and qualities, and then began to make nineteenth-century musical sense of the score.

As I was working away, deep in the intricate task of becoming an orchestrator, a monk passed through the room and saw me. He was one of several authorities in the place. "Why don't you get to work like the rest of us," he said gruffly, "instead of playing around at the piano."

In my home now I have a page from an illuminated manuscript, framed, hanging on a wall. I look at that page, at the green plant painted in the hollow of the large "P" in the words *Parce mihi, Domine*—Spare me, O Lord—and I realize that monks sometimes forget that their proper work is art and play, and I still pray that I will be spared the criticism of the moralist who disapproves of my wanton ways.

$\mathcal{W}$HEN I THINK OF WHY PEOPLE BE-
come monks I can think of no good reasons. One man's
father had tried to be a monk and failed, and so his son tried
to complete the job, much to the son's sorrow and frustra-
tion. Another was gay and hoped to find companionship in
the male environment of the monastery. I, myself, was led
to monastic life when, at a vulnerable age, I idolized the
boys who were my seniors and who had left home for the
monk's life.

Could it be that, at least sometimes, good things come
from wrong reasons?

NCIENT TEXTS THAT OFFER GUID-
ance to monks often advise ways to resist the temptations of
sex. What is it about sex that is inimical to the monk's life?
The obvious answer is the monk's need for solitude; yet one
gets the impression from the early texts that the issue lies
deeper.

Sex tugs at the monk and invites him down into related-
ness, pleasure, and the complications of romantic involvement. His aim is toward a loftier life of considerable sub-
tlety and simplicity.

The intensification of sex as a quintessential temptation,
complete with preoccupying thoughts and fantasies, is yet
another paradox in monastic life. It places the monk in
extraordinary dialogue with his sexual nature, and in that
sense he is more involved in sex than he would be without
his vow.

Flight usually intensifies the very thing one flees, and
establishes a special intimacy with it.

$\mathcal{M}$EDIEVAL STORIES ABOUT MONKS frequently tell of brothers breaking the rules in order to acquire money. Why would a person be a monk, and at the same time break the very rules that establish the life he has freely chosen?

Rules only make sense if they are both kept and broken. Breaking the rule is one way of observing it.

The monk abandons the values of the greater society, as does the criminal, yet, in breaking the rules, one becomes a saint and the other a sinner.

*W*HEN I WAS A NOVICE, THE MONAStery where I lived had an orchard filled with a wide variety of apples. On weekends we brothers would load a wagon full of cider and apples, and take it to the road to sell to passersby. I always enjoyed driving the tractor and hearing the corks pop off the bottles that were filled with the more aged cider.

We had apples for every occasion. One variety, the Wolf River, was unusually large, brilliantly red, and symmetrically shaped. Customers couldn't stop themselves from buying these apples, even though I would explain to them that this fruit had very dry meat and was the worst kind we had for eating.

There is something odd about a monk trying to convince innocent people not to eat the bright red apple.

WHAT IS A MONASTERY WITHOUT A heavy, thick, wooden door! In every monastery where I lived the monks generally used back doors and side doors made of metal or painted wood. It always felt strange to enter by the main door, as though it were too serious for daily use. Doors always invite a rite of passage, but especially doors of considerable weight and woodenness.

One of the most mysterious things a person can do is to knock on a monastery door and enter through that portal. It's like walking through a looking glass or finding the entrance to a cave that opens into a hidden world.

Life is filled with such doors, some real and some metaphorical. Some are likely thresholds of the soul, while others are astonishingly improbable.

*I*T IS SAID THAT PICO DELLA MIRANDOLA, the Renaissance philosopher who in his mid-twenties called the world to Rome to debate his ideas, planned to write a book on poetic theology. This book has yet to be written and its idea still to be fully realized.

The artist who works in dialogue with the muse is perhaps the best theologian, and the theologian who thinks, speaks, and writes poetically the most reliable source of religious knowledge. History gives us many attempts to link art and religion, yet it is always our task, in the most ordinary and individual ways, to find one in the other.

The truly artful life, not the merely aesthetic one, is religious, and vice versa.

A litany of thanks to these scribes and others who brought this book quickly into print:

 To Michael Katz, who knows monks and books

 To Hugh Van Dusen, who knows the world and retreat
   from the world

 To Father Patrick McNamara, man of wit and spirit and
   master of all of us novices

 To Pat Toomay, a brother of a different order

 To David Bullen, who plies the ancient trade of making
   precious books

 To Joan Hanley, who loves things into beautiful existence

 To Abraham and Siobhán, who are still close to the angels